6

Winter
Stranger

Winter Stranger

poems

Jackson Holbert

MILKWEED EDITIONS

Published 2023 by Milkweed Editions
Printed in Canada
Cover design and illustration by Mary Austin Speaker
23 24 25 26 27 5 4 3 2 1
First Edition

Library of Congress Cataloging-in-Publication Data

Names: Holbert, Jackson, author.
Title: Winter stranger : poems / Jackson Holbert.
Description: First edition. | Minneapolis, Minnesota : Milkweed
Editions, 2023. | Summary: "Jackson Holbert's Winter Stranger is a
solemn record of addiction and the divided affections we hold for the
landscapes that shape us"-- Provided by publisher.
Identifiers: LCCN 2023001105 (print) | LCCN 2023001106 (ebook) |
ISBN 9781639550418 (hardback) | ISBN 9781639550425 (ebook)
Subjects: LCSH: Drug addiction--Poetry. | LCGFT: Poetry.
Classification: LCC PS3608.O482873 W56 2023 (print) | LCC
PS3608.O482873 (ebook) | DDC 811/.6--dc23/eng/20230110
LC record available at https://lccn.loc.gov/2023001105
LC ebook record available at https://lccn.loc.gov/2023001106

Milkweed Editions is committed to ecological stewardship. We strive
to align our book production practices with this principle, and to reduce
the impact of our operations in the environment. We are a member
of the Green Press Initiative, a nonprofit coalition of publishers,
manufacturers, and authors working to protect the world's endangered
forests and conserve natural resources. *Winter Stranger* was printed on
acid-free 100% postconsumer-waste paper by Friesens Corporation.

for Olivia

and for my parents

Contents

For Jakob · 1

I

2003 · 4
We Learned the Mountains by Heart · 5
The Christmas Poem · 6
Letter from Nine Mile · 7
Letter Sent and Subsequently Returned by
    the Mailman · 8
These White Letters Look Nothing Like
    the Snow · 11
For Taylor · 14
The 26th Birthday Poem · 16
The Lamps · 17

II *The Book of Jakob*
Unsent Letter to Jakob · 21
Another Winter Poem · 22
Jakob in the Basement · 25
Another Summer Withdrawal Poem · 27
Waking in the City · 29
Unfinished Letter to Jakob · 31
Poem with a Smoke Cloud Hanging in It · 33
After Rilke · 35

Poem · 36
One Last Poem for Jakob · 37

III

World War I Poem · 41
World War I Poem · 43
Evil Nature · 45
January · 46
Fragment · 47
Burying the Dead High Up on the
    Mountain · 48
Love Poem to the Terrible Doctors · 50
Poem Containing No Pills · 51
After C.D. Wright · 52
Dream Where the Men Are in My House,
    Eating My Food, and Stealing My Ideas · 53

IV

Landscape · 57
The Water Poem · 58
Two Pastoral Poems · 61
The Uncle Poem · 63
Moth · 68

Notes · 69
Acknowledgments · 71

The earth loved us a little I remember
—RENÉ CHAR,
translated by MARY ANN CAWS

Winter Stranger

For Jakob

When we travel
the dead travel too.

That is the law
and the law is full of dreams.

It's April. We're dying
again, all of us, among poplars,

among blueberries and hail
hard as ball bearings.

The news says
wildfires are burning

all over the county.
I wake

from the couch
I've been sleeping on

for weeks. I put on
my grayest shoes,

blow ash off the deck
with a hose. I sit

in the yard
and close my eyes.

I left that town
forever. I dreamed,

rarely, of streams,
of blackbirds. I drew

everything we did
to the trees,

everything the trees
did to us.

I drew it badly
and spent years trying

to draw it well. Eventually,
I stopped.

I

2003

Say a girl
two towns over
beats a cat to death with a padlock
and goes to bed
Say you've loved the girl for years
and you want her to lay you down
and count your knuckles in the dark
and she wants you to lay her down
and wring the salt water
out of her blue hair
Say sorrow is a place
filled with people
and cars
and the ruins of mountains
and pine needles the color of your mother's hair
Say the hawks wheeling above the river
are just hawks
Say it to the hawks

We Learned the Mountains by Heart

We went to school we ate pink beef we drank
lots of water we snorted ritalin our nostrils
turned red we lifted weights we killed a mama moose
we sold her teeth online we poked each other's
muscles we laid our large bodies down on
docks and smelled the wind we bucked
hay our skin was hard we touched our palms
together speeding down the highway we turned
the headlights off and felt a little holy we were strong
but we were thin we slept on couches
we tore rotten stumps with our big hands we swaddled
our little sisters we wrestled our dogs we punched
each other in the kidneys we shinnied up
magnolias we closed our eyes we watched
moonlight spread across the snow
we went to church we pelted magpies off
the cherry trees we trapped a spider and then we let him go

The Christmas Poem

there are thousands of days left
tens of thousands if we're lucky and dozens
of new pills to try Merry Christmas look at the light
crashing thru the blackout curtains the cars
slide by and the suburbs disappear Prius by Prius
there is a father chopping lettuce there
is a mother shoveling snow there is
frostbitten wildgrass starving in the valleys
and there are cabins filled with families and cabins empty
except for the cold there is a baker walking
to her midnight shift there is a tall mayor
thanking donors there are dozens of winter suns left
and thousands of prisoners writing letters
reading letters there is a courthouse in the snow there
is a country everywhere and there are roads and towns
and courthouses and glowing Walmarts
and power lines everywhere and the notion of winter
falls everywhere even in California it descends
even when we can't see it it is like moonlight tonight
the snow looks like crushed pills and I don't care about trees
or mayors or bakers or fathers I care about the snow—
how grim it is in the dark and how quiet in the light

Letter from Nine Mile

Last night coyotes yipped the dogs into a frenzy.
Smoke and wind and toads croaking out
their proud, weird songs.
The black river. The small stars.
I've started to remember my dreams—
it's night, March snow
covers the hills. Last week, a boy named James
dove into the river north of here. Four miles
downcurrent, a farmer
fished out his small, blue body.
Outside my window, a crane breaks
the last jigsaw of ice. Morning comes,
it always does, the rabbits scurry down
their narrow holes to their underground lives.
They pip up in the sun, then
pip back down. I walk too long.
It keeps the stars circling. I run my fingers
along the tops of weeds. Every night a hundred crows
perch on the power lines and scream.

Letter Sent and Subsequently Returned
by the Mailman

Every now and then
in the middle of the night
I take my whitest sheet of paper
out of the closet
and begin
another letter to you. But this time it won't
be written on a page torn
out of a book, won't be written
with a carpenter's pencil
I found in a parking lot
somewhere in the north of Oregon.
This time I will sit at my huge desk
and not on my oversized bed.
Most of the time I write nothing,
even when I try my hardest,
but when I do get something down
I scratch it out then lay the paper
in the burn pile along with the credit card offers
and franked mail.
I have tried
every day. I promise that. It's just
that so many of my letters
have come to nothing and even those I did manage
to finish and drop in the outbound mailbox
were rejected by the postman

for reasons still unknown to me
even though I put many stamps on them,
so many, possibly too many. If you are as very far from me
as I think you are then it means winter is already
where you are, which means that the
cemeteries are already coated
with snow and the plowmen from
the outlying towns have billeted
themselves in the city center
and you know how I hate plowmen,
always knocking over the mailboxes
of upstanding citizens,
always pulling out in front of me
on my way to the Olive Garden.
They wouldn't stop for a hitchhiker
even if the hitchhiker was just a baby
with his baby thumb out
waiting in his carriage in the rain.
I'd stop for that baby.
When I try to focus
on the letters my mind moves away
contemptuously fast.
It's like holding a rope attached
to the bumper of a truck
that's about to pull out
onto the highway.
There is some pleasure
in these letters, I do not mean
to conceal that,

though I fear that I have.
Do not think that my life is all
fuck fuck fuck fuck fcuk fuck1!!!1!11
I promise there is joy
even if, at times, it feels
like it has been refracted
through a window, that
some meaningful fragment
has been lost on its way to me.
Before I try to write I put on
my good pants and my pressed shirt,
which brings us—me and my
letters—a little joy
and gives me a good excuse
to use the iron.
You'd think with all the reading I've done
along the way
I'd be able to write anything out with near perfect
accuracy and yet here we are
nearing the center of another page,
my lines coming nowhere near the right-hand margin
and the letter disappearing so rapidly behind me.

These White Letters Look Nothing
Like the Snow

You arrived
in the middle
of the long failure
of my youth
the bad grades
the locked doors and repeated
punches to my own head
just above the hairline
so if I did bruise
and I never bruised
they would have to hold
a flashlight to my hair
to see the damage.

Afterwards I was always
so worried
about what my fists were doing what
indefinite damage
they were enacting
to my child brain
but then playing
football in the 7th grade
I got hit hard and fell
headfirst
into the early winter grass

and discovered all those punches
had been nothing discovered
that I could do much
worse than that
and remain alive.

But how was I
supposed to know
that death doesn't
have to leave a mark
to come and go
at any hour
of the day or night,
that some years he
sends just his fingers
toward you
and some years he sends
his entire body
to sit gently
on the bed beside you.

But more than anything
how was I supposed to know
that for all those years
I thought myself dying
death was so much farther off
than I thought
that he was only
visiting my apartment

albeit day after
day and it was
the kicking of my own weak legs
that left my feet
sore each morning
and not death
making its way out of the earth
and into my heart.

For Taylor

A few miles upriver
Taylor walked through the parking lot
of the new high school
and put a bullet through his skull.
The whole baseball team saw.
Because of the way the valley is shaped
you could hear the sirens for a long time.

When I got to the funeral
S and K were already there,
speaking softly in big coats
on the cement steps
of the otherwise white church.
The three of us walked inside together.

When a thing is gone forever
you don't hold on to it,
that's just not true. You watch it
turn weightless and bizarre
and slip through your large hands
and into the earth forever.
So instead of knowing where it lies
instead of letting it sleep
beside your husband,
sleep beside your child,
you sense it only now and then

and by surprise when you get the mail
or walk the dog. And you're never sure
if it stopped sinking long ago
or if it kept going,
the way fertilizer poisons the aquifer
miles and miles down.

The 26th Birthday Poem

Five years ago almost to the day,
I watched the month
decay around me
from a porch in Boston,
watched the morning shift leave for work
and lock their doors behind them.

If you had told me then
how many nights
I would have stayed up,
how many days
I would have slept through.

A long life full of terror
is still a long life. And the terror
subsides after a little while
until you can barely distinguish it
from the clouds. (I promise.)

The Lamps

You are holding
a lamp and I
am holding a lamp.

We are talking about
other people,
people who are not
holding lamps.

I know they left you
at home. Did not even
extend to you
the kindness
of leaving you behind
at a bus depot,
a train station.

This is why
I am here
holding a lamp
beside you in the dark.

Drunk on the November lake
the quiet trees lean out
over the dirty water your cheap
pleasure craft sadly trills.

Do not forget I am here.
And do not think that I hold
this lamp for your sake alone.

But we must extinguish them
for a few hours.
We must let the boat drift
for its own sake. We must attend
our lives even in the dark.

II

The Book of Jakob

Unsent Letter to Jakob

When the pills entered my life
I knew what to do, but I didn't
know what to do when they stayed.
On a Saturday, last winter,
the light changed. Every color
backed away into the past and became
all at once, incoherent, immutable.
There is no explaining it. All I know is that
it was like the seizure you had
on the baseball field in the dark—
neither of us could stop it. And I'm not sure
if I'm interested in stopping it. Not anymore.
Though I think of you all the time
my memories still vanish like salt.
God knows what is doing the vanishing—
my vague and everwidening
psychoses, the pills themselves. Someday soon
I will lose your hair, your ears, your hands,
the color of your car, the first names
of your parents, and what's left
after that? The fucked up
trees? The long, cold river?

Another Winter Poem

as if it was not uncommon at all
the birds starting
to make themselves heard
on the unfit ice
as if moving away
from a thing was not
the same as moving
toward an end as
if what we had in us
after all
was the will to end
as if driving
together through town
at eighteen summer's
last thunder behind us by miles
soaking the boaters
and filling the sloughs
was a signal
that a thing of great
significance had or was
occurring like when you're looking
out over the lake and there's
one helicopter and then another

as if to be alone
together was some gift

we would have to give back
and not some gift
that would lodge in us
for far too long

as if to curse that life
was not to curse this life

if we were proof
of anything
then we were proof
of the sunlight
how after
it penetrates the earth
it keeps going
but slowly

as if proof mattered and could
not be destroyed
as easily as ice

all that fall
in the long wake we were making of our lives
the birds woke up
eye by eye
and flew south

they could smell
I think
the winter

when you see some things
for the first time
you know you have to go

but it takes seeing them
over and over
to know how and where and when.

Jakob in the Basement

I am done with your dead eyes,
done with your hospital grip socks
and white laceless shoes.
I am done with everything
that touches you,
but I am not done
with you, you who further whiten with each winter.
I am doing my best
to bring you up
out of the basement,
but I owe you nothing but love
and the love I owe you weighs
exactly what your thinning body weighs.
I am getting you out of here
even if it takes the whole night,
even if I have to call up all
our old friends. My plan
is this—when it gets
just dark enough
for passing truckers
to mistake us for lovers,
I will leave your heavy,
sweat stained jacket
on the unpatterned tile
although the cold has
come down from the trees

and place your arm
around my neck
and limp us both
toward your white Pontiac.

Another Summer Withdrawal Poem

We must arrive
at the long hours
of our suffering.

We must live within them.
They will not be there
to make this cease.

They will not be there
to chalk a line
down the pavement

that ends somewhere.
But we must live
within them. They will rise

and keep rising and fork out
like lightning
over the blank prairie.

Only in the worst minutes
will we hear our death
bending behind us in fits

like a thick sheet of paper
the printer
is testing the grain of.

And we will ask
our death to face us
but it will not face us.

And we will try to turn around
but our death
will disappear like snow

falling into snow.
There will be no suits
in this new life.

There will be no black shoes.
There will be nothing
left to save us.

Waking in the City

Your nights, King, your nights
—RILKE, translated by EDWARD SNOW

Your nights.
I can feel them now only
in the music of passing cars.

It's all so intricate
and so long, the way two lives
move in tandem till they don't,

the way two people live
together in a kingdom
of their own making,

a kingdom they carry
from apartment
to apartment and later

from house to house in boxes
the size of couch cushions, boxes
the size of televisions.

And then one day
while they sleep, the kingdom
will move away

from this world. The two false kings
will wake well after dawn
in a graying city,

a city they hadn't
noticed for years.
Outside their house

it will be spring and crowds
will be moving slowly
down the block

toward some festival
or parade. The two people
will comb each other's hair out

and put on their best clothes
and walk into the scenery
which is now their lives.

Unfinished Letter to Jakob

And I
left like
so many
stunned fish, so
many dull,
uncataloged moons.
It doesn't always
come back to you,
but some
weeks I wish
it did. We were both
at fault. Why
did you ever think
otherwise? I didn't
stop you. You
didn't stop.
Starving wild under
a Seroquel sky
the September of
your first overdose I
thought constantly
of fruit—plums,
blackberries, plums.
I knew I could
have them all
if I could only

reach you, but
I never tried, aware
all along that
although my hunger
might darken like
a frightful vein,
it would never
eat me alive as long
as you, somewhere, lived.

Poem with a Smoke Cloud Hanging in It

Today I will sit
in the grass and smell
the sunlight. I will leave
the pills in their bottles,
I will leave the bottles
by my bed. I will walk
to the insane river. I will let
the crazy wind cut and curve
around me. I will close
my eyes and dream
of medical sewage
poisoning the river a hundred
miles upstream. And somewhere
in all that trash
there is a little hit
of morphine. I will think
if nothing ever leaves
then the wind is full
of all the smoke I ever blew.
And if nothing ever leaves
does that mean I'm still
dopesick at fifteen, telling
my parents the flu is going around?
If I am then so what.
I am also walking through the cemetery
at dawn, friends

on both sides of me—our little
drunken army marching
out of the night.
If I am, then so what. I am also
lying in my bed at twenty-two staring
so deeply at the bark beetle-riddled trees
that I don't notice
the vacant light lessening then
leaving entirely. I don't notice
when the night climbs into my bed
like a terrified brother and the wind
slams the door.

After Rilke

The birds here sing when light touches them.
In the courtyard I think of the dealer
whose clients are all dead, his voice
so lonely only the rain will help. Recently,
the pictures in the locked ward seem
to back away from me, as if they know
you're there too. And just today
I saw, in one of the ever-recurring
paintings of saints that line the long
halls, the uncertain light that filled
all those childhood afternoons and evenings
when we were so afraid.

Poem

For me, you will always be eighteen, standing
in the halls of your parents' house,
your mother yelling for dinner, the whole country
out the window behind you, our whole
strange country laid before us in the way
a king lays his knives on the table.

One Last Poem for Jakob

It is clear now that there are no ends, just winters
that seem to settle then, when the time comes,
vanish without us through the wide summer windows.
The light doesn't even end when it hits
the tree, the grass, the river. It just spreads, changes,
and at most grows white. I thought a world after you
would be a world without you, but there you are
within the wood, within the water, you who
have always gotten into everything, even the sugar.

III

"And then I began to think about history"
—ANNE CARSON

World War I Poem

Everything depends on boys who know nothing,
who can barely make their beds,
who still need their mothers
to do almost anything.
The country depends on them,
senators, kindergarteners,
mailmen depend on them,
those boys standing in the rain,
the creases in their hats
filling almost comically with water.

Once the photograph is taken
the boys walk away. They sit alone
on barrels, museum steps,
or lean against the faces of brick buildings.

This is the real shot—the boys
mulling around, quiet.

Even from this far away
it's clear they won't last long,
these boys
in their autumn coats and shined shoes,
it's clear that something
has already gone

terribly wrong,
something only dead boys can fix,
and thousands of them.

World War I Poem

All through the war
there's no singing,
then one day
everyone's singing.

And we are unprepared, the friends
of the dead, we who wake now
without reason while all about us
cars fly by sailing little

flags, little stupid flags,
while children sing
through the broken windows
of provincial churches.

Everyone knows that the bones
go away faster without marrow,
that a god, outmoded and outdefined,
cannot manage every fixture of the day

and so gives each day allotments
of sound, light, pain,
meaning when there were great bombardments
the whales went silent,

when rifle regiments with ancient names
raised their weapons to the sky
and fired hopelessly at scouting planes
someone, dying alone

suddenly found himself
unable to scream. And the sound
that's left after that, the thin ribbons
not eaten up by rifle fire

move through us in waves—
miracle waves, dread waves—and the gone
feel nothing, say nothing, which means
the children can sing a little louder.

Evil Nature

after Eluard

All around us the dead are shackled
to radiators,
bedposts, flagpoles. The constant
artillery fire clacks their teeth
together, which keeps away
the mice.
What few birds remain
fly at night
when the artillery is loudest.
The owls, which are so large
you can make them out,
even in the dark,
have begun to assemble
in unheard of formations,
formations that resemble
extinct words, stray cats, white trees.

January

never twilight
never the entire river

the old blood
hides in the old

heart, cling
to me

when we are dead,
blue, the French language
will be of no use to us

graciously
you give my suffering

a name
graciously

my suffering
gives itself another

Fragment

As if to begin some process
that at its end yields
simply another summer with or
without you in it in another life
with or without you in it
in which the rocks
have always been hollow
and the stale snow stays all season.

Burying the Dead High Up on the Mountain

after Adrienne Rich

So I guess you're not
coming home again
with me. Snow falling
through dire-sleep,
mountain-sleep. Snow
falling all around you,
snow that turns to rain
as you descend, having taken
my pocketknife to give
to my mother, who, knowing
the body could not be brought back,
asked only for some small souvenir
of her child's long death.
And everything from now on a hunkering
behind boulders wide as horses,
everything a staunch crouch
to keep away the cold.
There are great forces in front of me
and greater forces behind me.
Cirques the size of cities, false ridges,
rock routes that do not end, or end in pure
precipice. All the minor peaks
are littered with minor people,
and the great peaks

with snow. Come to me
if you want. Through the Kyrgyz light,
the Tajik light, come and find me.
I feel you and your shovel
moving up the mountain.
I feel warm tea brewed at dawn
as the ice splinters all around us.
I feel you learning meekly,
step by step, what happens
when the cold you thought
you were given, the cold
you thought would move through you
and leave behind only a little branching damage,
a little scarring of the nerves, stays.

Love Poem to the Terrible Doctors

O play doctor play doctor we are
as antique leaves or Cynthia trees
working our roots toward the great house
where the children sleep with all the lamps
blown out. And you are singing,
which means I am singing, which
means the Cynthia trees must be shaking
even through these long, still days.
The doctor comes into the terrible house
and when he leaves he comes into the trees,
and for a terrible moment is the trees.
Which means we were the doctor. And that
is not my life. What I do is live
in the dark with you. And I
will be there with you as the pumpkins
fatten on the vine and the cold sweeps
each precinct with snow. The ice
will change nothing. Doctors of fingernails
doctors of fibulas doctors of the dirty snow.
Before winter is through they will
wade into the snow and draw
their saws of bone and cut us through
although they were never meant to.

Poem Containing No Pills

Although I cannot
remember you coming
through the wheat every
Sunday evening I can
say that even
in the worst years
I would have lent you horses.
And after a terrible day
I would have led
half of them down
to the lake with you
to drink the awful water
that tastes like pencils.

After C.D. Wright

I need a curtain and some lemonade,
spiders for friends, and a nice

lawn to have my visions on. I should
have never let that church buy my father's

piano for slightly under market value.
I should have taken the contents

of my mother's fridge when I had the chance.
I would be thin no longer nor young

if I had done the things I should have done.
If the best among the least of all the trees

I planted long ago to brace
the hillsides against strong rain

still stand after this spring, I'll fill my best glass
with water, and put on a little music.

Dream Where the Men Are in My House, Eating My Food, and Stealing My Ideas

The men smell like watches.
Their mothers smelled like watches too.
It was one of those men who woke me,
gently, with the hand on which he did not
wear his watch. He led me downstairs.
Eight men were arguing around the dinner table
about the hiring practices of the Home Depot on
    Fourth and Broadway.
There was a ninth in the corner
reading the biggest newspaper I'd ever seen.
It was the kind of morning where you just knew there'd
    be ice
hanging all over the trees. Later the tallest one
told me he thinks it's funny that if he hits me hard enough
I won't ever make it back to Tennessee.

IV

Landscape

Poisonous rivers make
poisonous ice.
In every mailbox
for a dozen miles
there's the same letter.
But the crows still bite through
the skin of the best
honeycrisps. The apple ladders
lean without suspicion.

I have no trouble believing
in any of this. The snow comes down
hard. It is spring.

I could keep saying this forever
and still nothing would be preserved.

The Water Poem

Somewhere north of here
my uncle grinds an oxycodone
into a thousand red granules.
Somewhere north of here
my uncle is dead and dark thunderheads
force the pleasurecraft to shore.
I can make it all sound so beautiful.
You'll barely notice that underneath
this poem there is a body
decaying into the American ground.
I can say clear coat, burnward.
I can say pleasurecraft all night long.
I can make his life or my life
or your life remarkable
if you give me a notebook
and a few unstructured days.
I can make it mean so much.
But I'm done with all that—
I've done death's handiwork before.
This time I'm coming home.

I swear this isn't all about water,
although I know it may come off that way.
There's something to the river's
indifference. What else would let in a baby
but keep out the lightning?

When I was a baby I almost died.
It didn't have anything to do
with the river, but it did
have something to do with my uncle.
While my dad and I were visiting him
in the courtyard
of the Airway Heights Corrections Center
I dawdled away—unnoticed—
from the lines of visiting families,
the guards with their small gauge shotguns,
and pulled a black mushroom from the tallgrass
and ate it. At the hospital
they pumped my tiny stomach
for 37 minutes. Outside the rain
started going crazy and by the time we left
through the automatic exit doors
my parents were so worried
the bridge would wash out
that we sat in the car for five hours
with the country station on.

But that's all fire under the bridge.
It's only now that I realize
I've written so many poems
with rivers inside of them
and never even mentioned history—
how it determines everything
and how it is what the water displaces first.
Rivers don't remember anything—
that's what makes them rivers.

Two Pastoral Poems

1

spring came
and so did summer
and a Halloween filled
with dirty snow

when I walked outside the world looked like
newspaper

beneath me
the frozen lightning
of the sycamore roots

it is late November
and I count everything now

there is the night and there
is the strange, dark river

there is the tremendous, awful land

and there is the mailman with his white letters

2

I fear the canyon
and where it leads

when I was twelve I found a lodestone
and I went to the creek and I buried it in the creekbed

year by year the treeline climbed

what I remember now of winter
is white birds on white horses

and asking the epileptic cow
to show me all of its teeth

The Uncle Poem

avuncular
trees
or was it avuncular skyscrapers?
yea it was the skyscrapers but
I don't know man
I remember it was Tuesday
the cars were doing their
normal car shit some asshole
was blasting Puccini
out of his BMW and some other
asshole was singing
an opera as he walked
down Main Street
what else
I saw my grandmother
this wasn't anything crazy
she's still alive
she lives in town she was
driving her convertible
very slow I waved at her but
I'm not sure she recognized me
no other family interactions to report
something about the day unsettled me tho
in the worst way possible
I knew I would be going home soon
home to the hills where

hill things happen
but I had thrown that terror into the future
like a baseball or a bag of trash
and of course it is the future now but I'm not
in the hills not yet
so why were the skyscrapers
avuncular to me
me who had many uncles none
of whom were skyscrapers
I think I have a few less uncles
now but it's hard to keep track
big family and you know what
they say uncles are like crab apples they wither
maybe it was that it
smelled like crab apples
while I walked down Main Street
I don't know where
that quote comes from probably
someone famous but I remember my uncle
saying it and it seems like a quote
about your uncles dying but that uncle
wasn't dying not yet he was
very much alive and very much
addicted to oxycodone
but the consequences would be
far in the future but I guess
the future is now which means
the consequences have already happened

which makes perfect sense
because that uncle died
tho not of overdosing exactly he died
of a heart attack induced by fireworks
on the Fourth of July one of three
citizens to do so in the county that day I
do not know what made hearts
so angry on that particular Fourth it was warm
but when wasn't it
warm in the valley I wasn't
there when my uncle died I
had picked up overtime
at the call center I have
determined that he is the uncle
I am referring to when I said
the skyscrapers were avuncular
tho referring isn't the right word
I didn't intend to call them avuncular
I felt it and it wouldn't go away
like a dog bite
but what made the skyscrapers
so avuncular my uncle had never been
to the city and possibly had never been
to any city he was country from his hair to the tip
of each toe he was so country that his countryness
    stretched
out from his body and into his car
maybe it's because he never

saw these skyscrapers that I
think of him tho that
is bullshit and I know it so why the fuck
could I not push the avuncular
skyscrapers out of my decidedly
non-avuncular brain
was it the windows? the
black paneling?
maybe it isn't the building at all
maybe it's the idea of the building
and tho I don't believe in ideas
I do believe in uncles
maybe it is that the building
is so high it would take minutes to elevator up
and maybe an hour to climb
which means by the top you would be in
the future the real future the future minutes
away not seconds a future farther than
a word is from another word and maybe
because I look
at the skyscraper from the top down
I think of those elevators in reverse
which means I think of the future in reverse
and if those elevators go enough
the future will reverse enough to be the past
like the real past
like a few months ago when my
uncle was breathing and taking

pills and feeling the high
come on like television static
turning into TV or like TV
turning into television static

Moth

after Chessy Normile

it would be nice to hear you say
that maybe the microphones have been on the whole time,
that the rooms we walked through
years ago picked up our conversations,
that not everything was lost just after it was said.

Notes

Charles Wright's poem "The Bolivar Letters, 4" contains the phrase "Play doctor, O play doctor."

The title construction "One Last Poem For . . ." is taken from Sandra Cisneros's "One Last Poem for Richard." "For Jakob" first appeared in *Four Way Review*.

"2003" first appeared, in an altered form, in *Willow Springs*.

"We Learned the Mountains by Heart" first appeared in *The Nation*.

"The Christmas Poem" first appeared in *Guernica*.

"Letter from Nine Mile" first appeared in *Colorado Review*.

"Two Pastoral Poems" and "Poem with a Smoke Cloud Hanging in It" first appeared in *Narrative*.

"January" first appeared in *Cincinnati Review*.

"Unsent Letter to Jakob," "The Uncle Poem," and "Love Poem to the Terrible Doctors" first appeared in *Poetry*.

Acknowledgments

My council of war: Avigayl Sharp, Lo Green, Soeun Seo, Hedgie Choi, Amelia 3300.

For friendship, teaching, and everything in between—

The Brandeis University English and Creative Writing Departments, particularly Elizabeth Bradfield, Olga Broumas, and William Flesch.
The faculty, staff, and students at the Michener Center for Writers.
The faculty, staff, and students at the New Writers Project.
The faculty, staff, and fellows of the Stanford University Creative Writing Program.
The Stadler Center for Poetry & Literary Arts.

Emily Duggan, Grace Gallagher, Elaine Mancini, Acacia England, Marcia Moore, Jack Newport, Natasha Trethewey, Robert Hass, John Darnielle, Beth Kessler, Isabelle Edgar, Tuesday Utz, Mary Calo, Craig Baranowski, Ariana Yeatts-Lonske, Alecia Sing, Matt Sullivan, Adam Lemon, John Whalen, William Weare, Melissa Superville, the Gunther family, the Manning family, the Mancini family.

I'd also like to thank Joanna Klink, Sarah Matthes, Mary Szybist, and J. Bailey Hutchinson for the attention they gave to this manuscript.

Louise Glück, for believing in these poems.

And Henri Cole, for selecting this book. Thank you.

photo: Ula Lucas

JACKSON HOLBERT was born and raised in eastern Washington. His poems have appeared in *Narrative*, *The Nation*, and *Poetry*. He received an MFA in Poetry from the Michener Center for Writers. He is currently a Stegner Fellow at Stanford and lives in Oakland, California.

The sixth award of the
MAX RITVO POETRY PRIZE

is presented to
JACKSON HOLBERT

by

MILKWEED EDITIONS
and
THE ALAN B. SLIFKA FOUNDATION

Designed to honor the legacy of one of the most original poets to debut in recent years—and to reward outstanding poets for years to come—the Max Ritvo Poetry Prize awards $10,000 and publication by Milkweed Editions to the author of a debut collection of poems. The 2022 Max Ritvo Poetry Prize was judged by Henri Cole.

Milkweed Editions thanks the Alan B. Slifka Foundation and its president, Riva Ariella Ritvo-Slifka, for supporting the Max Ritvo Poetry Prize.

milkweed
EDITIONS

Founded as a nonprofit organization in 1980,
Milkweed Editions is an independent publisher.
Our mission is to identify, nurture, and publish
transformative literature, and build an engaged
community around it.

Milkweed Editions is based in Bdé Óta Othúŋwe
(Minneapolis) within Mní Sota Makhóčhe, the
traditional homeland of the Dakhóta people. Residing
here since time immemorial, Dakhóta people still
call Mní Sota Makhóčhe home, with four federally
recognized Dakhóta nations and many more Dakhóta
people residing in what is now the state of Minnesota.
Due to continued legacies of colonization, genocide,
and forced removal, generations of Dakhóta people
remain disenfranchised from their traditional
homeland. Presently, Mní Sota Makhóčhe has become
a refuge and home for many Indigenous nations and
peoples, including seven federally recognized Ojibwe
nations. We humbly encourage our readers to
reflect upon the historical legacies held in
the lands they occupy.

milkweed.org

Milkweed Editions, an independent nonprofit publisher, gratefully acknowledges sustaining support from our Board of Directors; the Alan B. Slifka Foundation and its president, Riva Ariella Ritvo-Slifka; the Amazon Literary Partnership; the Ballard Spahr Foundation; *Copper Nickel*; the McKnight Foundation; the National Endowment for the Arts; the National Poetry Series; and other generous contributions from foundations, corporations, and individuals. Also, this activity is made possible by the voters of Minnesota through a Minnesota State Arts Board Operating Support grant, thanks to a legislative appropriation from the arts and cultural heritage fund. For a full listing of Milkweed Editions supporters, please visit milkweed.org.

Interior design by Mary Austin Speaker
Typeset in Caslon

Adobe Caslon Pro was created by Carol Twombly
for Adobe Systems in 1990. Her design was inspired by
the family of typefaces cut by the celebrated engraver
William Caslon I, whose family foundry served
England with clean, elegant type from the early
Enlightenment through the turn of the
twentieth century.